_____

Is the hilarious owner
of this book.

~ The Challenge ~

Read through the book & try to remember as many jokes as you can.

- - - - - - - - - - - - - - -

Tell at least one joke a day to your friends or family using just your memory.

- - - - - - - - - - - - - - -

Check off each joke in the book. Then, keep going until you've checked off all the jokes and become a master joke-teller!

~ Joke Telling Tips ~

Practice the joke by saying it out loud to yourself.

Remember to speak clearly and slowly.

Don't worry if you make a mistake or forget a part of the joke - just keep going and have fun!

Pause at the punchline to build up suspense.

Always end your joke with a big smile and enjoy the laughter with your friends!

2

Knock Knock

Who's there?

Shore.

Shore who?

Shore hope you like bad jokes!

Knock Knock

Who's there?

Barbie.

Barbie Who?

Barbie Q Chicken!

 **Knock Knock** ☐

Who's there?

 **An interrupting cow**

An interrupt—

SHOUT

 **MOOOOOOOO!**

Knock Knock

Who's there?

Boo

Boo who?

Don't cry, it's just a joke!

 Knock Knock

Who's there?

 Lettuce.

Lettuce who?

 Lettuce in, it's cold out here!

Knock Knock □

Who's there?

 Candice.

Candice who?

 Candice door open, or what?

Knock Knock

Who's there?

Dishes.

Dishes who?

Dishes the police, open up!

 **Knock Knock**

 **Who's there?**

 **Cows.**

Cows who?

 **Cows go "moo," not "who!"**

Knock Knock

Who's there?

Broken pencil.

Broken pencil who?

Oh, forget it. It's pointless!

 **Knock Knock**

 Who's there?

 Tank.

 Tank who?

 You're welcome!

 **Knock Knock**

Who's there?

 Dozen.

Dozen who?

 **Dozen anybody want to let me in?**

Knock Knock

Who's there?

Avenue.

Avenue who?

Avenue heard this one before?

Knock Knock

Who's there?

Spell.

Spell who?

W. H. O.

 **Knock Knock**

 Who's there?

 Cash.

 Cash who?

 No thanks, I prefer peanuts.

 **Knock Knock**

Who's there?

 Figs.

Figs who?

 Figs the doorbell. I've been knocking forever!

Knock Knock

Who's there?

Interrupting sloth.

Interrupting sloth who?

(20 seconds of silence)
Sloooooooooth.

 **Knock Knock**

 Who's there?

 Stopwatch.

Stopwatch who?

 Stopwatch you're doing and let me in!

 **Knock Knock**

Who's there?

 **Woo.**

Woo who?

 **Glad you're excited too!**

Knock Knock ☐

Who's there?

Tennis.

Tennis who?

Tenn-is five plus five.

 **Knock Knock**

Who's there?

 **Watts.**

Watts who?

 Watts for dinner?
I'm hungry.

Knock Knock

Who's there?

Who.

Who who?

I didn't know you were an owl!

Knock Knock

Who's there?

Ketchup.

Ketchup who?

Ketchup with me, and I'll tell you!

Knock Knock

Who's there?

Needle.

Needle who?

Needle little help opening the door!

 **Knock Knock**

Who's there?

 **Goat.**

Goat who?

 **Goat to the door and find out!**

Knock Knock

Who's there?

Beets.

Beets who?

Beets me!

 **Knock Knock** ☐

Who's there?

 **You.**

You who?

 **Yoo-hoo! Anybody home?**

 Knock Knock

Who's there?

 Butter.

Butter who?

 Butter let me in or I'll freeze!

 **Knock Knock**

Who's there?

 Radio.

Radio who?

 Radio not, here I come!

 **Knock Knock** □

Who's there?

 **Zoom.**

Zoom who?

 **Zoom did you think it was?**

Knock Knock

Who's there?

Sue.

Sue who?

Sue-prize! Happy birthday!

Knock Knock

Who's there?

Wendy.

Wendy who?

Wendy door bell gonna start working again?

33

 **Knock Knock**

Who's there?

 **Noah.**

Noah who?

 **Know a place I can spend the night?**

Knock Knock

Who's there?

Nobel.

Nobel who?

Nobel ... that's why I knocked!

Knock Knock

Who's there?

Ice cream.

Ice cream who?

 SHOUT

ICE CREAM, SO YOU CAN HEAR ME!

 **Knock Knock**

Who's there?

 **Anita.**

Anita who?

 **Anita use the bathroom, please open the door!**

Knock Knock

Who's there?

Canoe.

Canoe who?

Can-you come out now?

 **Knock Knock**

Who's there?

 Olive.

Olive who?

 **Olive you sooooo much!**

 **Knock Knock**

Who's there?

 Ears.

Ears who?

 Ears another knock knock joke for ya!

Knock Knock

Who's there?

Luke.

Luke who?

Luke through the peephole and find out.

Knock Knock

Who's there?

Kanga.

Kanga who?

Actually, it's kangaroo!

 **Knock Knock** ☐

Who's there?

 **Ya.**

Ya who?

 **Yippee!**

 **Knock Knock** ☐

 Who's there?

 Honey bee.

Honey bee who?

 Honey bee a dear
and get the door
for me.

Knock Knock

Who's there?

Icy.

Icy who?

Icy you in there!

Knock Knock

Who's there?

Alex..

Alex who?

Alex-plain later, just open up!

 **Knock Knock**

Who's there?

 **CD.**

CD who?

 **CD person knocking on the door?**

Knock Knock

Who's there?

Ben.

Ben who?

Ben knocking for 10 minutes!

 **Knock Knock**

Who's there?

 Cargo.

Cargo who?

 Car go "Toot toot, vroom, vroom!"

Knock Knock

Who's there?

A little old lady.

A little old lady who?

Hey, I didn't know you could yodel!

Knock Knock

Who's there?

Hatch.

Hatch who?

Bless you!

Knock Knock

Who's there?

Nana.

Nana who?

Nana your business!

Knock Knock

Who's there?

Snow.

Snow who?

Snow use. The joke is over.

Knock Knock

Who's there?

Leaf.

Leaf who?

Leaf me alone!

54

 **Knock Knock**

Who's there?

 **Razor.**

Razor who?

 **Razor hands, this is a stickup!**

 **Knock Knock**

Who's there?

 Wooden shoe.

Wooden shoe who?

 Wooden shoe like to hear another joke?

Knock Knock

Who's there?

Amish.

Amish who?

Really? You don't look like a shoe!

 **Knock Knock**

Who's there?

 **Voodoo.**

Voodoo who?

 **Voodoo you think you are?**

 **Knock Knock**

 Who's there?

 Cher.

 Cher who?

 Cher would be nice if you opened the door!

59

 **Knock Knock**

Who's there?

 Cows go.

Cows go who?

 No silly, cows go MOO!

 **Knock Knock**

Who's there?

 Mikey.

Mikey who?

 Mikey doesn't fit in the key hole!

Knock Knock

Who's there?

I am.

I am who?

You don't know who you are?

 **Knock Knock**

Who's there?

 Justin.

Justin who?

 Justin the neigh-bourhood and thought I'd come over!

 **Knock Knock**

Who's there?

 Owls say.

Owls say who?

 Yes, they do!

 **Knock Knock**

 Who's there?

 Europe.

 Europe Who?

 **No, YOU're a poo!**

Knock Knock

Who's there?

Haven.

Haven who?

Haven't you heard enough of these knock-knock jokes?

Knock Knock

Who's there?

Carl.

Carl who?

A Carl get you there faster than a bike!

 **Knock Knock**

 Who's there?

 Robin

 Robin who?

 Robin you! Now hand over the cash.

 **Knock Knock**

Who's there?

 Champ.

Champ who?

 Sure, but don't forget conditioner.

 **Knock Knock** ☐

Who's there?

 **Gorilla.**

Gorilla who?

 **Gorilla me a hamburger!**

Knock Knock ☐

Who's there?

Oink oink.

Oink oink who?

Are you a pig or an owl?

 **Knock Knock**

Who's there?

 Ice cream soda.

Ice cream soda who?

 Ice scream soda people can hear me!

Knock Knock

Who's there?

Amos.

Amos who?

A mosquito!

Knock Knock

Who's there?

Anudder.

Anudder who?

Anudder mosquito!

 **Knock Knock**

Who's there?

 Icing.

Icing who?

 Icing so loudly so everyone can hear me!

Knock Knock

Who's there?

Pecan.

Pecan who?

Pecan someone your own size.

 **Knock Knock**

Who's there?

 **Cabbage.**

Cabbage who?

 **You expect a cabbage to have a last name?**

 Knock Knock

Who's there?

 Lettuce.

Lettuce who?

 Lettuce in or we'll break down the door!

Knock Knock

Who's there?

Four Eggs.

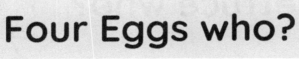

Four Eggs who?

Four Eggs ample.

 **Knock Knock**

Who's there?

 **Soup.**

Soup who?

 **Soup-er man.**

Knock Knock

Who's there?

Waffle.

Waffle who?

Stop waffling around and open the door.

Knock Knock

Who's there?

Art.

Art who?

R2-D2!

 **Knock Knock**

 Who's there?

 Tiss.

 Tiss who?

 A tiss-who is for blowing your nose.

 **Knock Knock**

 **Who's there?**

 **Beats.**

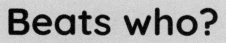 **Beats who?**

 **Beats me.**

Knock Knock

Who's there?

Frank.

Frank who?

Frank you for being my friend.

 **Knock Knock**

Who's there?

 **Smellmop.**

Smellmop who?

 **Ew, no thanks!**

 **Knock Knock** □

Who's there?

 **Says**

Says who?

 **Says me, that's who!**

Knock Knock

Who's there?

Police.

Police who?

Police hurry, I've got to go to the bathroom.

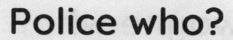

88

Knock Knock

Who's there?

 **Dwayne**

Dwayne who?

 **Dwayne the sink quickly before it overflows.**

 Knock Knock

Who's there?

 Interrupting pirate

Interrupting pira-

HOUT

 ARGHHHHHHHH

Knock Knock

Who's there?

Some.

Some who?

Maybe someday you'll recognize me!

Knock Knock

Who's there?

Billy Bob Joe Penny.

Billy Bob Joe Penny who?

Exactly how many Billy Bob Joe Pennies do you know?

92

 **Knock Knock**

 **Who's there?**

 **Caesar**

 **Caesar who?**

 **Caesar quick, she's running away.**

Knock Knock

Who's there?

Monkey.

Monkey who?

**Monkey see.
Monkey do.**

Knock Knock

Who's there?

Defense.

Defense who?

De-fense has a hole in it, so our dogs in your garden

 **Knock Knock**

Who's there?

 **Rough.**

Rough who?

 **Rough, rough! It's your dog!**

Knock Knock □

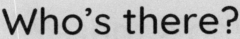
Who's there?

Alien.

Alien who?

Just how many aliens do you know?

Knock Knock

Who's there?

 **Sue.**

Sue who?

 **Sue-prize! It's me!**

98

 **Knock Knock**

Who's there?

 **Moustache**

Moustache who?

 I really moustache you a question but I will shave it for later.

 **Knock Knock**

 Who's there?

 Patsy.

Patsy who?

 Patsy dog on the head, he likes it.

Knock Knock

Who's there?

Doris.

Doris who?

Doris locked, that's why I'm knocking!

Knock Knock

Who's there?

Reed.

Reed who?

Redo? OK. Knock, knock. (Repeat from the start)

Thank you so much for your order. You just made my business grow, and for that, I am grateful!

If you enjoyed this book, please take a few moments to leave a review.

If you enjoyed this book, check out my other hilarious joke books!